Fantastic everyday Phonics practice from CGP!

CGP's Daily Practice Books are brilliant for building Phonics skills all the way through Year 1 — there's a mixed practice exercise for every day of the year.

What's more, they follow the National Curriculum 'Letters and Sounds' programme, so you can be sure they cover everything children need to learn.

This book is for the **Spring Term** of **Year 1**.

It covers part of **Phase 5** of the 'Letters and Sounds' programme, including:

- **Alternative pronunciations** for previously learned letters and letter combinations
- More **tricky words**

What CGP is all about

Our sole aim here at CGP is to produce the highest quality books — carefully written, immaculately presented and dangerously close to being funny.

Then we work our socks off to get them out to you — at the cheapest possible prices.

Contents

☑ Use the tick boxes to help keep a record of which tests have been attempted.

Week 1

- Day 1 1
- Day 2 2
- Day 3 3
- Day 4 4
- Day 5 5

Week 2

- Day 1 6
- Day 2 7
- Day 3 8
- Day 4 9
- Day 5 10

Week 3

- Day 1 11
- Day 2 12
- Day 3 13
- Day 4 14
- Day 5 15

Week 4

- Day 1 16
- Day 2 17
- Day 3 18
- Day 4 19
- Day 5 20

Week 5

- Day 1 21
- Day 2 22
- Day 3 23
- Day 4 24
- Day 5 25

Week 6

- Day 1 26
- Day 2 27
- Day 3 28
- Day 4 29
- Day 5 30

Week 7

- Day 1 31
- Day 2 32
- Day 3 33
- Day 4 34
- Day 5 35

Week 8

- Day 1 36
- Day 2 37
- Day 3 38
- Day 4 39
- Day 5 40

Week 9

- Day 1 41
- Day 2 42
- Day 3 43
- Day 4 44
- Day 5 45

Week 10

- Day 1 46
- Day 2 47
- Day 3 48
- Day 4 49
- Day 5 50

Week 11

- Day 1 51
- Day 2 52
- Day 3 53
- Day 4 54
- Day 5 55

Week 12

- Day 1 56
- Day 2 57
- Day 3 58
- Day 4 59
- Day 5 60

Published by CGP

ISBN: 978 1 78908 482 5

Written by Juliette Green

Editors: Daniel Fielding, Rebecca Greaves, Christopher Lindle, Sam Norman
Reviewer: Clare Leck

With thanks to Rosa Roberts and Lucy Towle for the proofreading.

Images throughout the book from www.edu-clips.com.

Printed by Elanders Ltd, Newcastle upon Tyne.
Based on the classic CGP style created by Richard Parsons.

How to Use this Book

This book is for children to complete in the Year 1 Spring Term. Each page looks like this:

The book is split into 12 weeks, with 5 days per week.

The box at the top of the page contains instructions. Read through these with your child and go through the worked example so they know what they're meant to do.

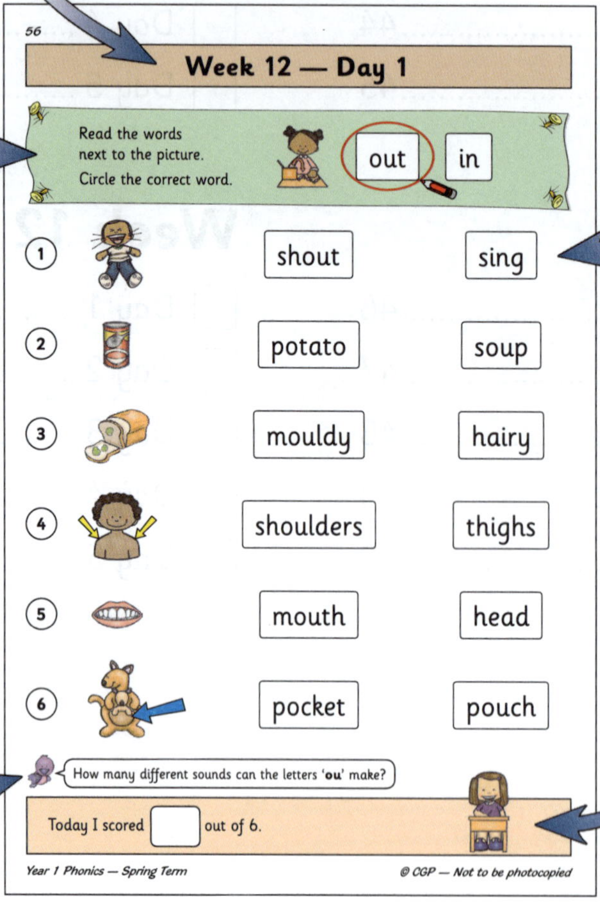
56

Week 12 — Day 1

Read the words next to the picture. Circle the correct word.

	out	in
1	shout	sing
2	potato	soup
3	mouldy	hairy
4	shoulders	thighs
5	mouth	head
6	pocket	pouch

How many different sounds can the letters 'ou' make?

Today I scored [ ] out of 6.

Year 1 Phonics — Spring Term

© CGP — Not to be photocopied

Talk your child through the first question. Each question follows the same format, so encourage your child to tackle the remaining questions independently.

You will need to read through the instructions for any extension activities.

The score box lets you keep track of how well your child is doing.

This book requires your child to match pictures to words.
You may need to help your child identify some pictures they're not sure of.

Phonics Hints for Helpers

Familiarise yourself with the features of this book below before you begin:

- Word frames are used in spelling and writing activities. There is one box for each sound. A sound can consist of more than one letter.

f	u	t	ure

- Tricky words are words with letters that have a sound that does not correspond to the expected sound, or that have a sound that has not yet been learned. Tricky words are written into blue boxes.

the | one | what

Week 1 — Day 1

Read the words next to the picture.
Circle the correct word.

child   gran

1 

sink   float

2 

snail   spider

3 

lost   winner

4 

bird   insect

5 

tiger   elephant

6 

lift   drop

How many different sounds can the letter 'i' make?

Today I scored ☐ out of 6.

Week 1 — Day 2

Read the words.
Draw a line to match each word to the best picture.

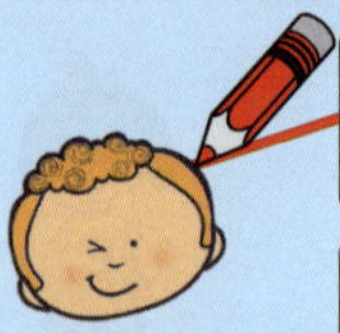

wink

mind

1

lion

spin

2

cockpit

pilots

3

wind

wind

4

driver

windmill

Today I scored ☐ out of 4.

Week 1 — Day 3

Read the word.

Then write a rhyming word in the word frame.

The picture will help.

skin

g r i n

1  silk  [ ][ ][ ][ ]

2  find  [ ][ ][ ][ ]

3  skill  [ ][ ][ ][ ]

4  grind  [ ][ ][ ][ ][ ]

5  think  [ ][ ][ ][ ][ ]

6  wild  [ ][ ][ ][ ]

Today I scored [ ] out of 6.

Week 1 — Day 4

Write the sentence in the word frames.

Do you like turkey?

Do | you | like | t ur k ey | ?

1. Come and have some cake.

2. The lions were so still.

3. She said there was a stink.

Today I scored ☐ out of 3.

Week 1 — Day 5

Read each sentence. Draw a line to match it to the best picture.

Oh no! There is a spider in my drink.

1 The children looked at us and said hi.

2 Mrs Timmins asked the kind child to help her.

3 Some people find that sleeping outside is fun.

4 Oh, what big ears and teeth you have!

5 The kids called their new pet Mr Tiger.

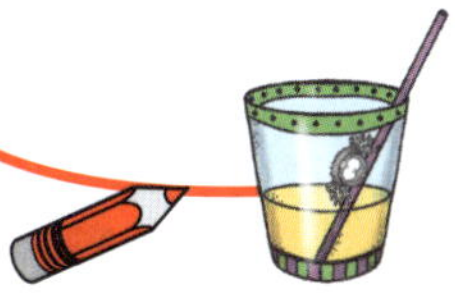

How many tricky words can you spot in these sentences?

Today I scored ☐ out of 5.

Week 2 — Day 1

Read the words next to the picture.
Circle the correct word.

lion | hippo (circled)

1 

roll | jump

2 

clock | troll

3 

otter | dolphin

4 

gold | silver

5 

clover | flower

6 

yo-yo | frog

How many different sounds can the letter '**o**' make?

Today I scored ☐ out of 6.

Week 2 — Day 2

Read the words.

Draw a line to match each word to the best picture.

over

open

1

cold

moth

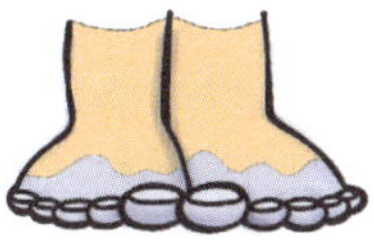

2

posting

jogging

3

photo

socks

4

daffodil

popcorn

Today I scored [ ] out of 4.

Week 2 — Day 3

Look at the picture.
Use the letter tiles to complete the caption.

o n

no food
or drinks

1

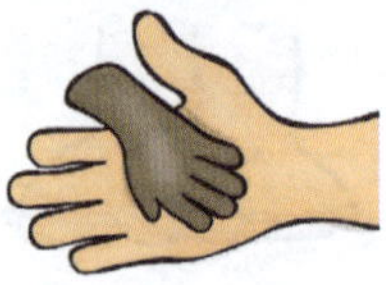

d l
o h

☐☐☐☐
my hand

2

g i
o ng

☐☐☐☐
up a ladder

3

o d l

an ☐☐☐
plane

4

o b th

☐☐☐
in stripes

Today I scored ☐ out of 4.

Week 2 — Day 4

Write the sentence in the word frames.

I don't eat meat.

I | d o n ' t | ea t | m ea t | .

Remember to put the apostrophe in '**don't**'.

1 We don't go near the old tower.

2 Insects don't like the cold.

3 Don't be so loud.

Today I scored [ ] out of 3.

Week 2 — Day 5

Read the sentence. Draw a line to match it to the best picture.

He ate too many cakes.

1. Many people get a cold in the winter.

2. She has so many dogs to feed at the shelter.

3. Many speakers use a microphone.

4. This king had many wives.

5. Many people don't like spiders.

Circle the tricky word '**many**' in these sentences.

Today I scored [ ] out of 5.

Week 3 — Day 1

Read the words next to the picture.
Circle the correct word.

ace | joker

1		sill	cell
2		pencils	crayons
3		ring	bracelet
4		December	June
5		zoo	circus
6		mermaid	princess

How many different sounds can the letter '**c**' make?

Today I scored ☐ out of 6.

Week 3 — Day 2

Read the word.

Then write a rhyming word in the word frame.

The picture will help.

ice

r	i	c	e

1  crown 

2  rocket 

3  mice 

4  race 

5  laces 

Today I scored ☐ out of 5.

Week 3 — Day 3

Look at the picture.
Use the letter tiles to complete the caption.

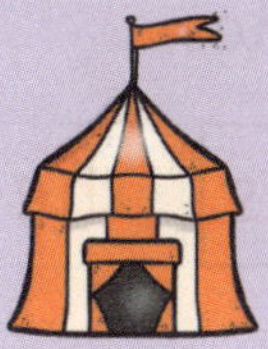

c c
u ir s

c	ir	c	u	s

tent

1 

c s p
a e

hopper

2 

c
i e

cream

3 

i n l
e p c

case

4 

c r
a e

wheelbarrow

Today I scored ☐ out of 4.

Week 3 — Day 4

Write the sentence in the word frames.

What is the price? | What | i s | the | p r i c e | ?

1. You can have a slice of cake.

2. Don't go down to the cellar.

3. He has a smile on his face.

Today I scored [ ] out of 3.

Week 3 — Day 5

Read each sentence. Draw a line to match it to the best picture.

She thought the bee might sting her.

1 Cecil the sea lion thought about his lunch.

2 The girls thought they might do some exercise.

3 Milo thought he might have a nap.

4 Carl thought the man might like some food.

5 I thought centipedes had 100 legs.

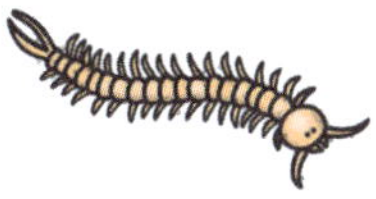

Circle the tricky word '**thought**' in these sentences.

Today I scored [ ] out of 5.

Week 4 — Day 1

Read the words next to the picture.

Circle the word that matches the picture.

book | page

1  cage | bird

2  Jack | giant

3  soft | rigid

4 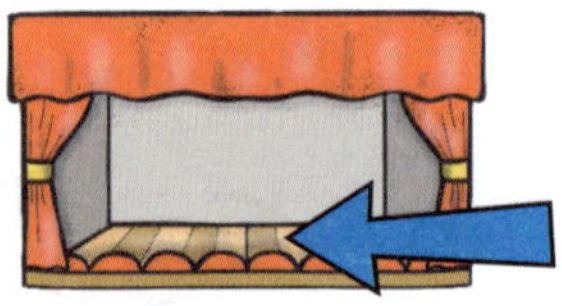 stage | curtain

5  huge | little

6 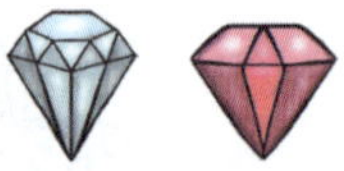 gems | acid

Today I scored ☐ out of 6.

Week 4 — Day 2

Read the words.
Match each word to the correct picture.

gel

girl

1

frog

rage

2

general

dragon

3

gate

germ

4

gerbil

eggs

Today I scored ☐ out of 4.

Week 4 — Day 3

Look at the picture.
Use the letter tiles to complete the caption.

le t
e g n

being
g e n t le

1

g n
i er g

made with
[ ][ ][ ][ ][ ]

2

a g
c m i

[ ][ ][ ][ ][ ]
beans

3

n g
e t

he is a
[ ][ ][ ][ ]

4

c g
a e

Gretel in a
[ ][ ][ ][ ]

Today I scored [ ] out of 4.

Week 4 — Day 4

Copy one of the words to complete the sentence.

He made a | little | igloo.

Practise writing the words first.

little one out

1. Gene went ______ onto the stage.

2. The ______ bird is in a cage.

3. ______ child is on the beanbag.

4. ______ germ got ______ of the lab.

5. I do a ______ bit of exercise each day.

Check you have used a capital letter for the first word in a sentence.

Today I scored ☐ out of 5.

Week 4 — Day 5

Read each sentence. Draw a line to match it to the best picture.

We had a water fight.

1 Plants need water to survive.

2 It's fun to splash in the water.

3 Water can be a liquid, a solid or a gas.

4 Fish have to stay in water or they will die.

5 There are water balloons in this bucket.

Circle the tricky word '**water**' in these sentences.

Today I scored ☐ out of 5.

Week 5 — Day 1

Read the words next to the picture.
Circle the correct word.

window | roof

1 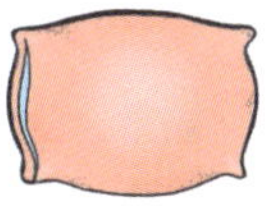 pillow | quilt

2  crown | robe

3  armpit | elbow

4  sunshine | rainbow

5 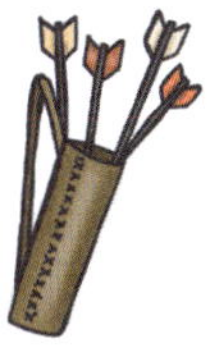 arrows | targets

6  smile | frown

7  show | flag

How many different sounds can the letters '**ow**' make?

Today I scored ☐ out of 7.

Week 5 — Day 2

Read the words.
Draw a line to match each word to the best picture.

towel

throw

1 

yellow

tower

2 

bow

bow

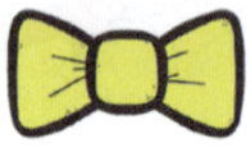

3 

crow

crowd

4 

rowing

rowing

Today I scored ☐ out of 4.

Week 5 — Day 3

Read the words.

Then colour in the word that has a different sound for the letters '**ow**'.

show	wow	tow

① brown | gown | blown

② cow | mow | now

③ bowl | owl | growl

④ snow | grow | how

⑤ slower | shower | flower

Today I scored ☐ out of 5.

Week 5 — Day 4

Write the sentence in the word frames.

Little snails are slow.

Little | s | n | ai | l | s | are | s | l | ow | .

1 Gill had a little yellow toy.

2 We have a little rowing boat.

3 The plane has little windows.

Today I scored ☐ out of 3.

Week 5 — Day 5

Read each sentence. Draw a line to match it to the best picture.

Yuck! I will never eat this again.

1 Lorenzo wants to go to the beach again.

2 She grew her hair long again.

3 The girl is going outside again.

4 We went to see the puppies again.

5 Lucian has sung that song again and again.

Circle the tricky word '**again**' in these sentences.

Today I scored ☐ out of 5.

Week 6 — Day 1

Read the words next to the picture.

Circle the correct word.

pie | cake

1.  thief | jail

2.  bow tie | hairband

3.  flies | fries

4.  arrow | shield

5.  painter | priest

6.  cherries | grapes

How many different sounds can the letters '**ie**' make?

Today I scored ☐ out of 6.

Week 6 — Day 2

Read the words.

Draw a line to match each word to the best picture.

shrieks

flies

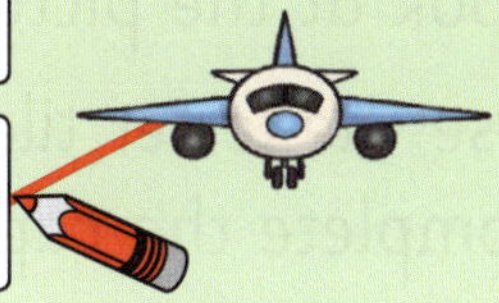

1

magpies

brownies

2

blueberries

families

3

stories

strawberries

4

hobbies

dries

Today I scored ☐ out of 4.

Week 6 — Day 3

Look at the picture.
Use the letter tiles to complete the caption.

c ie ll o

c	o	ll	ie

dog

1. 

f d ie l

of carrots

2. 

ie f ch

of the tribe

3. 

b e s rr ie

from a bush

4. 

c k s ie oo

a plate of

Today I scored ☐ out of 4.

Week 6 — Day 4

Write the sentence in the word frames.

My sister is one. → My | s i s t er | i s | one | .

1 One girl flies her kite.

2 Ollie has one pet goldfish.

3 Millie had one brief look.

Today I scored ☐ out of 3.

Week 6 — Day 5

Read each sentence. Draw a line to match it to the best picture.

Look through the keyhole.

1 He flies through the air like a bird.

2 Some people need to look through these.

3 Freddie has been crawling through a tube.

4 Melanie jumps through the hoop at the circus.

5 She slept right through her alarm.

Circle the tricky word '**through**' in these sentences.

Today I scored ☐ out of 5.

Week 7 — Day 1

Read the words next to the picture.
Circle the correct word.

meal | bowl

1. 

breakfast | bedtime

2. 

bleat | bark

3. 

dreaming | sweating

4. 

peach | beach

5. 

brief | breath

How many different sounds can the letters '**ea**' make?

Today I scored ☐ out of 5.

Week 7 — Day 2

Read the word.
Then write a rhyming word in the word frame.
The picture will help.

 seat  m | ea | t

1  beans 

2  head 

3  team 

4  weather 

5  thread 

6  heating 

Today I scored ☐ out of 6.

Week 7 — Day 3

Colour in the word that fits best into the sentence.

The | tea / peas | is in a pot.

1 

I have | read / eaten | this book.

2 

What a | dreadful / pleasant | day!

3 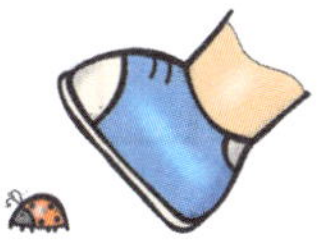

Don't | tread / heap | on that!

4 

He | dealt / heals | the cards.

Today I scored ☐ out of 4.

Week 7 — Day 4

Write the sentence in the word frames.

Put out the pasta. → P | u | t   out   the   p | a | s | t | a | .

1 Blake burst out of the hay.

2 Pixie was told to have time out.

3 Aleena took out the rubbish.

Today I scored ☐ out of 3.

Week 7 — Day 5

Read the question.
Then tick the box next to the correct answer.

Who has made bread?

a baker ☑
a driver ☐

1. Who is holding this balloon?

Ollie Owl ☐
Phil Pheasant ☐

2. Who is in the photo frame?

a pilot ☐
a girl ☐

3. Who is on the laptop?

a teacher ☐
a dentist ☐

4. Who is the pet inside the box?

Jake Snake ☐
Freddie Frog ☐

5. Who ate all of the breakfast?

Cinderella ☐
Goldilocks ☐

Circle the tricky word '**who**' in these questions.

Today I scored ☐ out of 5.

Week 8 — Day 1

Read the words next to the picture.
Circle the correct word.

hut | bush

1  sunset | sunflower

2  trumpet | tuba

3  bull | goat

4  brain | lung

5  rush | stroll

6  umbrella | unicorn

How many different sounds can the letter '**u**' make?

Today I scored ☐ out of 6.

Week 8 — Day 2

Read the words.
Match the words to the correct picture.

hull

mug

1

bulldog

human

2

skull

gull

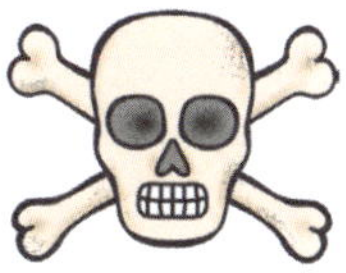

3

pulling

cutting

4

whoopie cushion

plum pudding

Today I scored ☐ out of 4.

Week 8 — Day 3

Look at the picture.
Use the letter tiles to complete the caption.

u m g

chewing
gum

1

i u
m s c

students

2

t u
f ure

in the

3

u n
o b tt

push the red

4

u ll f

he is so

Today I scored ☐ out of 4.

Week 8 — Day 4

Copy one of the words to complete the question.

When will the buds open up?

Practise writing the words first. In the sentences below they will all need to start with a capital letter.

When Do What

1. ______ cubs eat puddings?

2. ______ is this girl pushing?

3. ______ is it time for breakfast?

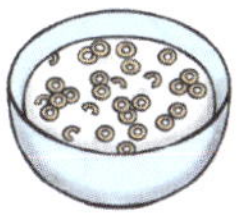

4. ______ exercise is this boy doing?

5. ______ unicorns exist?

Now tell someone else your answers to the questions.

Today I scored ______ out of 5.

Week 8 — Day 5

Read the question. Then colour the correct answer.

Where is the pig?

in the mud

on the bus

1. Where is Luna going?

swimming

shopping

2. Where are the kids playing?

on the beach

in a hut

3. Where is Bruno with his case?

at an airport

at the park

4. Where are these goldfish?

in water

on a chair

5. Where is the little bird?

in a nest

on a feeder

Circle the tricky word '**where**' in these questions.

Today I scored ☐ out of 5.

Week 9 — Day 1

Read the words
next to the picture.
Circle the correct word.

chin | chew

1 

parachute | balloon

2 

turkey | chicken

3 

headache | back ache

4 

chip shop | chalet

5 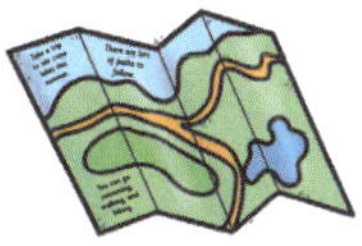

brochure | children

How many different sounds can the letters '**ch**' make?

Today I scored ☐ out of 5.

Week 9 — Day 2

Read the caption.
Then colour the correct picture.

church

① Christmas stocking

② anchor

③ a mixing machine

④ head chef

⑤ a book character

Today I scored ☐ out of 5.

Week 9 — Day 3

Use the letter tiles to complete the caption.

e | ch | ie | s | rr

a pair of

ch | e | rr | ie | s

1. ch | i | ar | ng | m

[| | | |]

with the band

2. ch | u | s | or

singing the

[| | |]

3. l | oo | ch | s

going to

[| | |]

4. or | s | d | ch

strumming

[| | |]

Today I scored [ ] out of 4.

Week 9 — Day 4

Write the sentence in the word frames.

When is it lunch? → When | i s | i t | l u n ch | ?

1. Be secure when you are in a car.

2. Chris had a nap when he got in.

3. This is when she went shopping.

Today I scored ____ out of 3.

Week 9 — Day 5

Read each pair of sentences. Draw a line to match it to the best picture.

Charlie is a chef.
Her work is cooking.

1. Malachi is a mechanic.
His work is fixing cars.

2. Nicholas is a conductor.
He works in an orchestra.

3. Charlotte is an architect.
Her work is technical.

4. Zach works in a school.
He is the cleaner.

5. Chelsea works at a chemist.
She is the pharmacist.

Today I scored ☐ out of 5.

Week 10 — Day 1

Read the words next to the picture.
Circle the correct word.

map | bank

1.  acorn | coconut

2.  bath | bacon

3.  father | sister

4.  bracelet | watch

5.  wasp | millipede

6.  trunk | branch

7.  apricot | banana

How many different sounds can the letter '**a**' make?

Today I scored ☐ out of 7.

Week 10 — Day 2

Read the caption.
Draw a line to match each caption to the best picture.

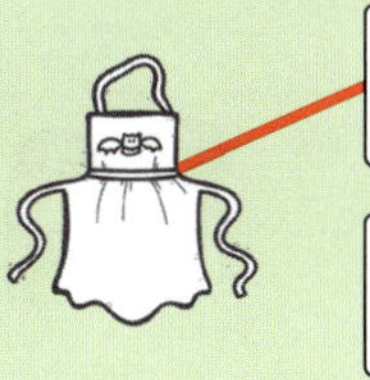

apron

mallet

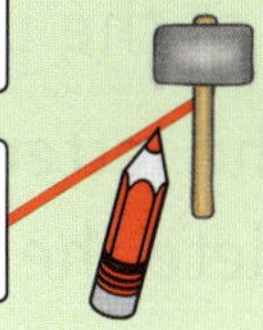

1

angel

swan

2

lampshade

grasshopper

3

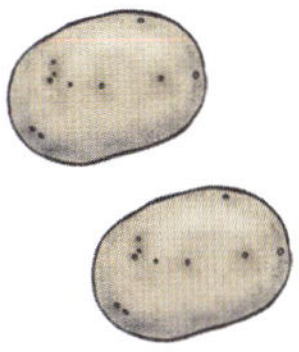

tomatoes

potatoes

4

ladies in hats

babies in nappies

Today I scored ☐ out of 4.

Week 10 — Day 3

Look at the picture.
Use the letter tiles to complete the caption.

a t l s

salt and pepper

1 

w i a ng sh

[ ] [ ] [ ] [ ] [ ] hands

2 

qu s a sh

glass of [ ] [ ] [ ] [ ]

3 

d n g er a

this sign means [ ] [ ] [ ] [ ] [ ]

4 

a p th

wander on the [ ] [ ] [ ]

Today I scored [ ] out of 4.

Week 10 — Day 4

Write the sentence in the word frames.

What is the time? → What | i s | the | t i m e | ?

① What do you want to do?

② You must do what she says.

③ Oh, what nice flowers!

Today I scored ☐ out of 3.

Week 10 — Day 5

Read each sentence. Draw a line to match it to the best picture.

Emil could not swim last year.

1. The squad could be the best next season.
2. Ruby could do over one hundred squats.
3. He could go so fast over the stepping stones.
4. The student could do all of the work.
5. The dog could rescue people from the snow.

Circle the tricky word '**could**' in these sentences.

Today I scored [ ] out of 5.

Week 11 — Day 1

Read the words next to the picture.
Circle the correct word.

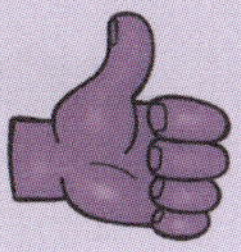

yew | yes

1 

yell | mystery

2 

why | sky

3 

crystal | strawberry

4 

smelly | carry

5 

reply | bicycle

6 

yoga | symbol

How many different sounds can the letter '**y**' make?

Today I scored ☐ out of 6.

Week 11 — Day 2

Read the caption.
Draw a line to match each caption to the best picture.

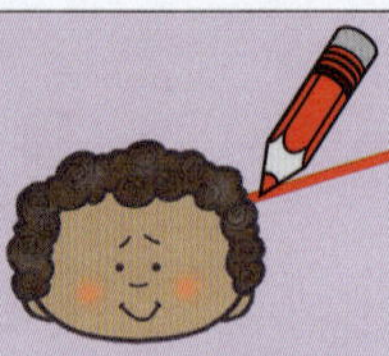

shy

heavy

1

yawn

cygnet

2

drying

spying

3

crunchy

sticky

4

pyramids in Egypt

an empty gym

Today I scored [ ] out of 4.

Week 11 — Day 3

Look at the picture.
Then tick the correct describing word.

Lily  happy ☐ grumpy ✔

1	yak		hairy	☐	tiny	☐
2	curry		funny	☐	spicy	☐
3	bunny		smelly	☐	yellow	☐
4	jelly		wobbly	☐	spiky	☐
5	puppy		woolly	☐	yappy	☐
6	penny		shiny	☐	stinky	☐
7	lolly		smoky	☐	icy	☐

Today I scored ☐ out of 7.

Week 11 — Day 4

Write the sentence in the word frames.

Do you fry eggs? | Do | you | f r y | e gg s | ?

1. I do try my hardest at maths.

2. I do want to marry you.

3. Do you cry at sad films?

Today I scored ☐ out of 3.

Week 11 — Day 5

Read each question. Draw a line to match it to the best picture.

Would you like some help?

1 Would you like a drink to give you energy?

2 Would you like to have a piggyback ride?

3 Would you like to dance with me?

4 Would you like him to keep the rhythm?

5 Would you like a sticky strawberry lolly?

Circle the tricky word '**would**' in these sentences.

Today I scored [ ] out of 5.

Week 12 — Day 1

Read the words next to the picture.
Circle the correct word.

out (circled) | in

1  shout | sing

2  potato | soup

3  mouldy | hairy

4  shoulders | thighs

5 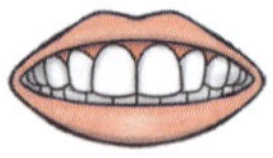 mouth | head

6  pocket | pouch

How many different sounds can the letters '**ou**' make?

Today I scored [ ] out of 6.

Week 12 — Day 2

Read the caption.

Draw a line to match each caption to the best picture.

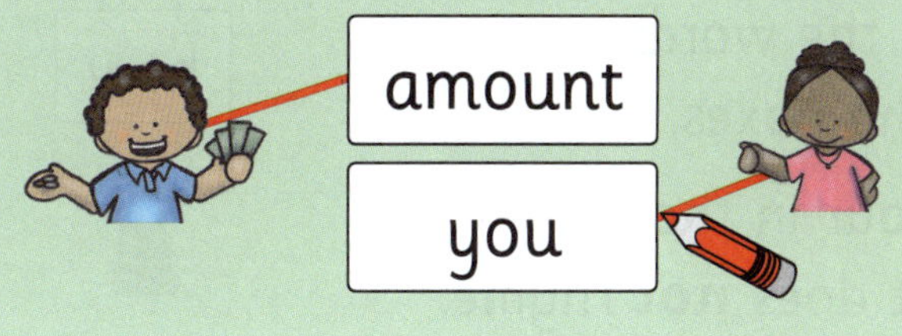

1 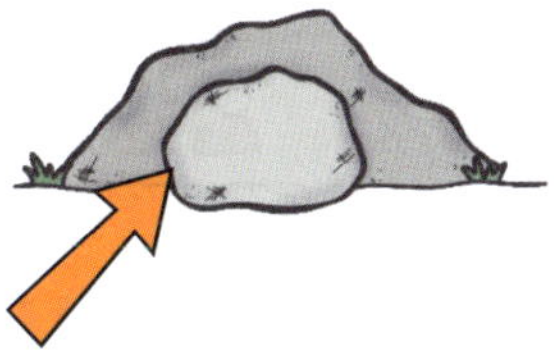

boulder

outside

2 

youth

group

3 

mounted

counted

4 

he could swim

she would cry

Today I scored ☐ out of 4.

Week 12 — Day 3

Say the words in the boxes.

Colour in the word that does **not** rhyme.

bow

how | wow | crow

1. mind

kind

find

wind

2. round

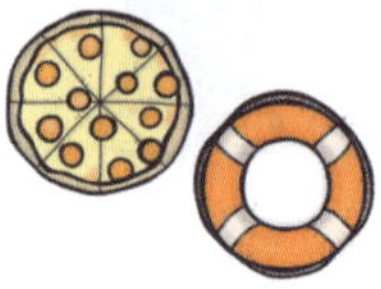

ground

wound

mound

3. throw

sow

grow

now

4. bread

lead

head

dead

Today I scored ☐ out of 4.

Week 12 — Day 4

Write your own sentence for each picture.

Use some of the sounds and tricky words you know.

She is laying the table.

Remember to use capital letters and full stops.

1

2

3

Today I wrote ☐ sentences.

Week 12 — Day 5

Read each sentence. Draw a line to match it to the best picture.

You should eat healthy food.

1. We should brush our teeth twice daily.

2. You should stay in bed if you feel unwell.

3. People should not feed the monkeys in the zoo.

4. You should wash your hands before eating.

5. Seeds should be given plenty of water.

Circle the tricky word '**should**' in these sentences.

Today I scored [ ] out of 5.

E1OWSP11